Daily Reflections on Life's Great Truths

Second Edition

By
Larry John Phillips

Published 2026 by Progressive Rising Phoenix Press, LLC
www.progressiverisingphoenix.com

ISBN: 978-1-958640-87-6

Printed in the U.S.A.
1st Printing

Cover Photo: "Beautiful Stunning Vast Tranquil Ocean." Stock Photo ID: 2451976713
By ShutterStock AI Generator. Image used under license from ShutterStock.com.

Book and Cover design by Amanda M. Thrasher and William Speir
Visit: http://www.williamspeir.com

January

1

All worthwhile men have good thoughts, good ideas and good intentions – but precious few of them ever translate those into action.

J. H. FIELD

Notes:

January

2

The difficulties and struggles of today are but the price we must pay for the accomplishments and victories of tomorrow.
WILLIAM J. H. BOETCKER

Notes:

January

3

Get the advice of everybody whose advice is worth having-they are very few - and then do what you think best yourself.

CHARLES STEWART PARNELL

Notes:

January

4

As for old age, embrace and love it. It abounds with pleasure if you know how to use it. The gradually declining years are among the sweetest in a man's life, and I maintain that, even when they have reached the extreme limit, they have pleasure still.

LUCIUS ANNAEUS SENECA

Notes:

January

5

The people who are crazy enough to think they can change the world are the ones who do.
STEVE JOBS

Notes:

January

6

No matter how much someone deserves your anger, the anger itself does not hurt that person as much as it hurts you.
NINA WALTER

Notes:

January

7

Do not look forward to what might happen tomorrow; the same Everlasting Father who cares for you today will take care of you tomorrow and every day. Either He will shield you from suffering, or He will give you unfailing strength to bear it. Be at peace then and put aside all anxious thoughts and imaginations.

FRANCIS DE SALES

Notes:

January 8

Appearances do not make the man, but it will pay any man to make the best appearance possible.
ROY L. SMITH

Notes:

January 9

Don't be stingy with words of appreciation when they are justly due. Everyone likes to be told that he is admired, respected, and appreciated, and liked.
NICOLAS CAUSSIN

Notes:

January

10

Your living is determined not so much by what life brings to you as by the attitude you bring to life; not so much by what happens to you as by the way your mind looks at what happens.

JOHN MILLER

Notes:

January

11

Another kind of beauty is possibly the highest type of all. Beauty of spirit, as revealed by the expression on the face of a human being. By the merry twinkle in the eye, by the smile on the lips – all indicating happiness and contentment within. This is probably the greatest beauty we will ever see.

WILLIAM ROSS

Notes:

January

12

When you arise in the morning, think of what a precious privilege it is to be alive – to breathe, to think, to enjoy, to love.

MARCUS AURELIUS

Notes:

January

13

When I consider what some books have done for the world, and what they are doing, how they keep up our hope, awaken new courage and faith, soothe pain, give an ideal; life to those hours are cold and hard, bind together distant ages and foreign lands, create new worlds of beauty, bring down truth from heaven; I give eternal blessings for this gift, and thank God for books.

JAMES FREEMAN

Notes:

January 14

Business is always a struggle. There are always obstacles and competitors. There is never an open road, except the wide road that leads to failure. Every great success has always been achieved by fight. Every winner has scars. The men who succeed are the efficient few. They are the few who have the ambition and the will-power to develop themselves.

HERBERT N. CASSON

Notes:

January 15

Calmness of mind is one of the beautiful jewels of wisdom. It is the result of long and patient effort in self-control. Its presence is an indication of ripened experience, and of a more than ordinary knowledge of the laws of thought.

JAMES ALLEN

Notes:

January

16

Surround yourself with people who make you happy. People who make you laugh, who help you when you're in need. They are the ones worth keeping in your life. Everyone else is just passing through.

KARL MARX

Notes:

January

17

The world hates change, yet it is the only thing that has bought progress.
CHARLES F. KETTERIN

Notes:

January

18

When wealth is lost, nothing is lost; when health is lost, something is lost; when character is lost, all is lost.

BILLY GRAHAM

Notes:

January

19

Cheerfulness is the great lubricant of the wheels of life. It lightens labor, diminishes difficulties, and mitigates misfortunes. Cheerfulness gives a creative power which the pessimist never possesses. A sunny, hopeful, optimistic disposition sweetens life, lightens its inevitable drudgery, and eases the jolts along the road.

COUNCILLOR

Notes:

January 20

This power to choose is what makes each one of us an individual, a god in his own right and our choices determine what happens to us – what our future will be – happy or unhappy, success or failure.

DAN CUSTER

Notes:

January

21

People are always blaming their circumstances for what they are. I don't believe in circumstances. The people who get on in this world are the people who get up and look for the circumstances they want, and if they can't find them, make them.

GEORGE BERNARD SHAW

Notes:

January

22

Neatness and cleanliness is not a function of how rich or poor you are but that of mentality and principle.

IKECHUKWU IZUAKOR

Notes:

January 23

True compassion means not only feeling another's pain but also being moved to help relieve it.
DANIEL GOLEMAN

Notes:

January 24

In every activity do your best and let the world make its own appraisement. You are what you are. Explanations seldom explain. Cultivate a fine sense of independence, based upon the assurance that you are loyal to a high standard conduct.

GRENVILLE KLEISER

Notes:

January

25

The proper development of self-confidence will be one of your most valuable assets. It will influence everything you do, whether you are in business or professional life. A full degree of self-confidence will enable you to occupy an important place, the place to which your talents entitle you.

GRENVILLE KLEISER

Notes:

January

26

A good conscience is a mine of wealth. And in truth what greater riches can there be, what thing more sweet than a good conscience.
ST. BERNARD

Notes:

January 27

Content has a kindly influence on the soul of man, in respect of every being to whom he stands related. It extinguishes all murmuring, repining, and ingratitude toward the Being who has allotted us our part to act in the world. It destroys all inordinate ambition; gives sweetness to the conversation, and serenity to all thoughts; and if it does not bring riches, it does the same thing by banishing the desire of them.

JOSEPH ADDISON

Notes:

January

28

It is amazing what you can accomplish if you do not care who gets the credit.
HARRY S. TRUMAN

Notes:

January 29

One ought never to turn one's back on a threatened danger and try to run away from it. If you do that, you will double the danger. But if you meet it promptly and without flinching, you will reduce the danger by half. Never run away from anything. Never!
WINSTON CHURCHILL

Notes:

January

30

Really big people are, above everything else, courteous, considerate and generous - not just to some people in some circumstances - but to everyone all the time.
THOMAS J. WATSON

Notes:

January

31

Imagination is the beginning of creation. You imagine what you desire, you will what you imagine, and at last, you create what you will.
GEORGE BERNARD SHAW

Notes:

February

1

Curiosity keeps leading us down new paths.
WALT DISNEY

Notes:

February 2

Then shall the dust return to the earth as it was; and the spirit shall return unto God who gave it.
BIBLE

Notes:

February 3

I have accustomed myself to receive with respect the opinions of others but always take the responsibility of deciding for myself.

ANDREW JACKSON

Notes:

February

4

Dependability is more important than talent. Dependability is a talent, and it is a talent all can have. It makes no difference how much ability we possess if we are not responsible and dependable.

FLOY L. BENNETT

Notes:

February

5

The real difference between man is energy. A strong will, a settled purpose, an invincible determination, can accomplish almost anything; and in this lies the distinction between great men and little men.

THOMAS FULLER

Notes:

February 6

We must suffer one of two things the pain of discipline or the pain of regret and disappointment.
JIM ROHN

Notes:

February

7

Develop a passion for learning. If you do, you will never cease to grow.

ANTHONY J. D'ANGELO

Notes:

February

8

The emotions are not always subject to reason…but they are always subject to action. When thoughts do not neutralize and undesirable emotion, action will.

WILLIAM JAMES

Notes:

February

9

The successful man has enthusiasm: Good work is never done in cold blood, heat is needed to forge anything. Every great achievement is the story of a flaming heart.

E. B. ZU TAVERN

Notes:

February

10

We believe, as asserted in the Declaration of Independence, that all men are created equal; but that does not mean that all men are or can be equal in possessions, in ability, or in merit; it simply means that all shall stand equal in the court of law.
WILLIAM JENNINGS BRYAN

Notes:

February

11

Great people have great values and great ethics.
JEFFREY GITOMER

Notes:

February

12

When it comes to health and well-being, regular exercise is about as close to a magic potion as you can get.

THICH NHAT HANH

Notes:

February

13

A prudent person profits from personal experience, a wise one from the experience of others.
DR. JOSEPH COLLINS

Notes:

February

14

Fairness is an across-the-board requirement for all our interactions with each other…Fairness treats everybody the same.
BARBARA JORDAN

Notes:

February

15

Thou shalt love thy Lord thy God with all thy heart,
and with all thy soul, and with all thy mind.
BIBLE

Notes:

February

16

Family and friendships are two of the greatest facilitators of happiness.
JOHN MAXWELL

Notes:

February

17

It's one of the greatest gifts you can give yourself, to forgive. Forgive everybody.

MAYA ANGELOU

Notes:

February

18

No one outside ourselves can rule us inwardly. When we know this, we become free.

BUDDHA

Notes:

February

19

You meet a person and you just click – you're comfortable with them, like you've know them your whole life, and you don't have to pretend to be anyone or anything.
ANONYMOUS

Notes:

February

20

Being frugal doesn't mean slashing your spending or depriving yourself of things that you enjoy. It means knowing the value of the dollar and making every effort to spend it wisely.

FRANK SONNENBERG

Notes:

February

21

Never let the future disturb you. You will meet it, if you have to, with the same weapons of reason which today arm you against the present.
MARCUS AURELIUS

Notes:

February

22

But I give best when I give from that deeper place;
when I give simply, freely and generously, and
sometimes for no particular reason. I give best when
I give from my heart.
STEVE GOODIER

Notes:

February

23

In the long run, the sharpest weapon of all is a kind and gentle spirit.
ANNE FRANK

Notes:

February 24

Gratitude unlocks the fullness of life. It turns what we have into enough, and more. It turns denial into acceptance, chaos to order, confusion to clarity. It can turn a meal into a feast, a house into a home, a stranger into a friend.
MELODY BEATTIE

Notes:

February

25

Excellence is an art won by training and habituation.
We do not act rightly because we have virtue or
excellence, but we rather have those because we have
acted rightly. We are what we repeatedly do.
Excellence, then, is not an act but a habit.
ARISTOTLE

Notes:

February

26

Most true happiness comes from one's inner life, from the disposition of the mind and soul. Admittedly, a good inner life is difficult to achieve, especially in these trying times. It takes reflection and contemplation and self-discipline.

W. L. SHIRER

Notes:

February

27

Look to your health; and if you have it, praise God, and value it next to a good conscience; for health is the second blessing that we mortals are capable of; a blessing that money cannot buy.

IZAAK WALTON

Notes:

February

28/29

He is happiest, be he king or peasant, who finds peace in his home.
JOHANN WOLFGANG VON GOETHE

Notes:

March

1

I hope I shall possess firmness and virtue enough to maintain what I consider the most enviable of all titles, the character of an honest man.

GEORGE WASHINGTON

Notes:

March 2

He has honor if he holds himself to an ideal of conduct though it is inconvenient, unprofitable, or dangerous to do so.
WALTER LIPPMANN

Notes:

March

3

There is no medicine like hope, no incentive so great, and no tonic so powerful as expectation of something better tomorrow.
ORISON SWETT MARDEN

Notes:

March

4

Whoever exalts himself will be humbled, and whoever humbles himself will be exalted.
BIBLE

Notes:

March

5

Good humor is a tonic for mind and body. It is the best antidote for anxiety and depression. It is a business asset. It attracts and keeps friends. It lightens human burdens. It is the direct route to serenity and contentment.

GRENVILLE KLEISER

Notes:

March 6

The American Dream is independence and being able to create that dream for yourself.
MARSHA BLACKBURN

Notes:

March

7

There is a higher court than courts of justice and that is the court of conscience. It supersedes all other courts.

MAHATMA GANDHI

Notes:

March

8

Be kind, for everyone you meet is fighting a battle
you know nothing about.
WENDY MASS

Notes:

March

9

KNOWLEDGE is power. It is nothing of the sort! Knowledge is only potential power. It becomes power only when if it is organized into definite plans of actions, and directed to a definite end.
NAPOLEON HILL

Notes:

March

10

I'd rather spend my leisure time doing what some people call my work, and I call my fun.
JARED DIAMOND

Notes:

March 11

To live content with small means; to seek elegance rather than luxury; and refinement rather than fashion; to be worthy, not respectable; and wealthy, not rich; to study hard, think quietly, talk gently, act frankly; to listen to stars and birds, to babes and sages, with open heart; to bear all cheerfully, do all bravely, await occasion, hurry never; in a word, to let the spiritual, unbidden and unconscious grow up through the common. This is to be my symphony.

WILLIAM HENRY CHANNING

Notes:

March

12

To love is nothing. To be loved is something. But to love and be loved, that's everything.
THEMIS TOLIS

Notes:

March

13

You cannot buy loyalty. You cannot buy the devotion of hearts, minds, and souls. You have to earn these things.
CLARENCE FRANCIS

Notes:

March

14

One of the signs of maturity is a man takes ownership of those things he does.
LARRY JOHN PHILLIPS

Notes:

March

15

It is circumstance and proper measure that give an action its character, and make it either good or bad.
PLUTARCH

Notes:

March

16

Two of the hardest things to accomplish in this world are to acquire wealth by honest effort and, having gained it, to learn how to use it properly.
ELMER H. BOBST

Notes:

March 17

One secret of success in life is for a man to be ready for his opportunity when it comes.
BENJAMIN DISRAELI

Notes:

March

18

The right mental attitude means a great deal. A mind filled with optimistic thoughts has no room for pessimism.
B. F. GIRARD

Notes:

March

19

Organization isn't about perfection; it's about efficiency, reducing stress and clutter, saving time and money, and improving overall quality of life.

CHRISTINA SCALISE

Notes:

March 20

May I forget what ought to be forgotten; and recall, unfailing, all that ought to be recalled, each kindly thing, forgetting what might sting.

MARY CAROLINE DAVIES

Notes:

March 21

Patience and perseverance have a magical effect, before which difficulties disappear, and obstacles vanish.

JOHN QUINCY ADAMS

Notes:

March 22

Resign every forbidden joy; restrain every wish that is not referred to God's will; banish all eager desires, all anxiety; desire only the will of God; seek him alone and supremely, and you will find peace.
FRANCOIS FENELON

Notes:

March

23

People only see what they are prepared to see.
RALPH WALDO EMERSON

Notes:

March 24

Most successes are built on failures. That is more than a paradox; it is an actual fact. Most successes have been built on failures, not on one failure alone but on several. A majority of the great historic accomplishments of the past have been the final result of persistent struggle against discouragement and failure. A man is never beaten until he thinks he is. Without perseverance, the chances of his succeeding are small indeed.

CHARLES GOW

Notes:

March 25

Nothing in this world can take the place of persistence. Talent will not; nothing is more common than unsuccessful people with talent. Genius will not; unrewarded genius is almost a proverb. Education will not; the world is full of educated derelicts. Persistence and determination alone are omnipotent. The slogan "press on" has solved and always will solve the problems of the human race.

CALVIN COOLIDGE

Notes:

March

26

The test of an enjoyment is the remembrance which it leaves behind.
JEAN PAUL RICHTER

Notes:

March

27

Your peers will respect you for your integrity and character, not your possessions.

DAVID ROBINSON

Notes:

March 28

The man without purpose is like a ship without a rudder; a waif, a nothing, a no-man. Have a purpose in life and having it, throw such strength of mind and muscle into your work as God has given you.

THOMAS CARLYLE

Notes:

March

29

Your reputation is in the hands of others. That's what reputation is. You can't control that. The only thing you can control is your character.

WAYNE W. DYER

Notes:

March

30

That you may retain your self-respect, it is better to displease the people by doing what you know is right, than to temporarily please them by doing what you know is wrong.

WILLIAM J. H. BOETCKER

Notes:

March

31

The price of greatness is responsibility.
WINSTON CHURCHILL

Notes:

April 1

Having purpose and vision during retirement is one of the most important determinants of mental, social, spiritual, and physical well-being in later life.
HAROLD G. KOENIG

Notes:

April

2

For a few minutes every day practice quietness. Choose a place where you can relax completely. Quietness and silence are a healing balm for a tired body and brain, frayed nerves, and needless foreboding.

GRENVILLE KLEISER

Notes:

April 3

The ability to simplify means to eliminate the unnecessary so that the necessary may speak.

HANS HOFMANN

Notes:

April

4

Sincerity of conviction and purity of motive will surely gain the day; and even a small minority, armed with these, is surely destined to prevail against all odds.

SWAMI VIVEKANANDA

Notes:

April

5

Solitude is important to man. It is necessary to his achievement of peace and contentment. It is a well into which he dips for refreshment for his soul. It is his laboratory in which he distills the pure essence of worth from the raw materials of his experiences. It is his refuge when the very foundations of his life are being shaken by disastrous events.

MARGARET E. MULAC

Notes:

April

6

Some days are just bad days, that's all. You have to experience sadness to know happiness, and I remind myself that not every day is going to be a good day, that's just the way it is.

DITA VON TEESE

Notes:

April

7

One ship drives east an another west, with the self-same winds blow; 'tis the set of the sails and not the gales that determines where they go. Like the winds of the sea are the ways of fate, as we voyage along through life; 'tis the set of the soul that decides it goal – and not the calm or strife.

ELLA WHEELER WILCOX

Notes:

April

8

Oh, fear not in a world like this, and thou shall know erelong, know how sublime a thing it is to suffer and be strong.

HENRY WADSWORTH LONGFELLOW

Notes:

April

9

The man who is born with a talent which he meant to use, finds his greatest happiness in using it.
JOHANN WOLFGANG VON GOETHE

Notes:

April

10

You are today where your thoughts have brought you, you will be tomorrow where your thoughts take you.

JAMES ALLEN

Notes:

April

11

Ordinary people think merely how they shall spend their time; a man of intellect tries to use it.
ARTHUR SCHOPENHAUER

Notes:

April

12

I do not like what you say but I will defend to the death your right to say it.
VOLTAIRE

Notes:

April

13

Trust in the Lord with all thine heart; and lean not unto thine own understanding. In all ways acknowledge him, and he shall direct thy paths.

BIBLE

Notes:

April 14

Truth matters supremely because in the end, without truth there is no freedom. Truth, in fact, is not only essential to freedom; it is freedom, and the only way to a free life lies in becoming a person of truth and learning to live in truth. Living in truth is the secret of living free.

OS GUINNESS

Notes:

April

15

Happy is the man that findeth wisdom, and the man that getteth understanding....her ways are ways of pleasantness, and all her paths are peace.... wisdom is the principal thing; therefore get wisdom; and with all thy getting get understanding.
BIBLE

Notes:

April

16

The only way to do great work is to love what you do.
STEVE JOBS

Notes:

April

17

Try first thyself, and after call in God, for to the worker God himself lends aid.
EURIPIDES

Notes:

April

18

A smooth sea never made a skillful mariner.
ENGLISH PROVERB

Notes:

April

19

The light that a man receiveth by counsel from another is drier and purer than that which cometh from his own understanding and judgement, which is ever infused and drenched in his affections and customs.

FRANCIS BACON

Notes:

April 20

I promise to keep on living as though I expected to live forever. Nobody grows old by merely living a number of years. People grow old only by deserting their ideals. Years may wrinkle the skin, but to give up interest wrinkles the soul.

DOUGLAS MACARTHUR

Notes:

April

21

There is one weakness in people for which there is no remedy. It is the universal weakness of lack of ambition.

NAPOLEON HILL

Notes:

April

22

A man is about as big as the things that make him angry.

WINSTON CHURCHILL

Notes:

April

23

Do not be anxious about tomorrow, for tomorrow will be anxious for itself. Let the day's own trouble be sufficient for the day.

BIBLE

Notes:

April

24

Charms strike the sight, but merit wins the soul.
ALEXANDER POPE

Notes:

April

25

The deepest principle in human nature is the craving to be appreciated.
WILLIAM JAMES

Notes:

April 26

The greatest discovery of my generation is that human beings can alter their lives by altering their attitudes of mind.
WILLIAM JAMES

Notes:

April

27

In all ranks of life the human heart yearns for the beautiful; and the beautiful things that God makes are his gifts to all alike.
HARRIET BEECHER STOWE

Notes:

April

28

We do not learn to value our blessings till we have lost them.

JOHANN GOTTFRIED VON HERDER

Notes:

April

29

In books we have the choicest thoughts of the ablest men in their best dress.

JOHN AIKIN

Notes:

April

30

Fortunes are built during the down market and collected in the upmarket.
JASON CALACANIS

Notes:

May

1

Nothing gives a person so much advantage over another as to remain always cool and unruffled under all circumstances.
THOMAS JEFFERSON

Notes:

May

2

Nobody cares how much you know, until they know how much you care.
THEODORE ROOSEVELT

Notes:

May

3

If you do what you've always done, you'll get what you've always gotten.
ANONYMOUS

Notes:

May

4

For when the One Great Scorer comes to write against your name, he writes - not that you won or lost - but how you played the game.
CHRISTINE RICE

Notes:

May

5

Joyous people are not only the happiest, but the longest lived, the most useful and most successful.
ORISON SWETT MARDEN

Notes:

May

6

You always do what you want to do. This is true with every act. You may say that you had to do something, or that you were forced to, but actually, whatever you do, you do by choice. Only you have the power to choose for yourself.

W. CLEMENT STONE

Notes:

May 7

Circumstances do not make a man; they only reveal him to himself.
JAMES ALLEN

Notes:

May

8

Cleanliness is a mindset – a positive habit that keeps the body, mind, and environment happy, healthy, simple, neat, and delightful.

AMIT RAY

Notes:

May 9

The greatness of man is measured by the way he treats the little man. Compassion for the weak is a sign of greatness.

MYLES MUNROE

Notes:

May

10

The virtue of man ought to be measured, not by his extraordinary exertions, but by his everyday conduct.
BLAISE PASCAL

Notes:

May

11

Fired by success – they could do it because they believed they could do it.
VIRGIL

Notes:

May

12

He will easily be content and at peace, whose conscience is pure.
THOMAS a' KEMPIS

Notes:

May

13

The secret of contentment is knowing how to enjoy what you have, and be able to lose all desire for things beyond your reach.

LIN YUTANG

Notes:

May

14

No matter how much work a man can do, no matter how engaging his personality may be, he will not advance far in business if he cannot work through others.

JOHN CRAIG

Notes:

May

15

Life shrinks or expands in proportion to one's courage.
ANAIS NIN

Notes:

May 16

Nothing is ever lost by courtesy. It is the cheapest of the pleasures, costs nothing and conveys much. It pleases him who gives and him who receives, and thus, like mercy, it is twice blessed.

ERASTUS WIMAN

Notes:

May

17

Imagination rules the world.
NAPOLEON BONAPARTE

Notes:

May

18

Blessed are the curious, for they shall have adventures.
ANONYMOUS

Notes:

May

19

If you would not be forgotten as soon as you are dead, either write things worth reading or do things worth writing.
BENJAMIN FRANKLIN

Notes:

May 20

When confronted with two courses of action, I jot down on a piece of paper all the arguments in favor of each one – then, on the opposite side, I write the arguments against each one. Then by weighing the arguments, pro and con, and canceling them out, one against the other, I take the course indicated by what remains.

BENJAMIN FRANKLIN

Notes:

May

21

Dependability is the base upon which all confidence rests in full security. Confidence may be termed the active result of basic dependability.

ROBERT E. HICKS

Notes:

May

22

In all human affairs, there are efforts, and there are results, and the strength of the effort is the measure of the result.

JAMES ALLEN

Notes:

May

23

No discipline seems pleasant at the time, but painful.
Later on, however, it produces a harvest of
righteousness and peace for those who have been
trained by it.
BIBLE

Notes:

May

24

Education is the key to unlocking the world, a passport to freedom.
OPRAH WINFREY

Notes:

May

25

When dealing with people remember you are not dealing with creatures of logic, but with creatures of emotion, creatures bristling with prejudice, and motivated by pride and vanity.
DALE CARNEGIE

Notes:

May

26

Flaming enthusiasm, backed up by horse sense and persistence, is the quality that most frequently makes for success.

DALE CARNEGIE

Notes:

May

27

All the citizens of a state cannot be equally powerful,
but they may be equally free.
VOLTAIRE

Notes:

May

28

Wrong is wrong, even if everyone is doing it. Right is right, even if no one is doing it.
WILLIAM PENN

Notes:

May

29

Physical fitness is not only one of the most important keys to a healthy body, it is the basis of dynamic and creative intellectual activity.
JOHN F. KENNEDY

Notes:

May

30

No one ever got good at anything by just reading a book about it. Real skill and improvement come from experience.

JUSTIN HAMMOND

Notes:

May

31

Win or lose, do it fairly.
KNUTE ROCKNE

Notes:

June

1

Ask, and it shall be given to you; seek, and you shall find; knock, and it shall be opened unto you.
BIBLE

Notes:

June

2

A happy family is just an earlier heaven.
SIR JOHN BOWRING

Notes:

June

3

To forgive is the highest, most beautiful form of love.
In return, you will receive untold peace and
happiness.
ROBERT MULLER

Notes:

June

4

Is freedom anything else than the right to live as we wish? Nothing else.
EPICTETUS

Notes:

June

5

Be civil to all; sociable to many; familiar with few; friend to one; enemy to none.
BENJAMIN FRANKLIN

Notes:

June 6

By sowing frugality, we reap liberty, a golden harvest.
AGESILAUS

Notes:

June

7

Go forth to meet the shadowy future without fear
and with a manly heart.
HENRY WADSWORTH LONGFELLOW

Notes:

June

8

Always give without remembering and always receive without forgetting.
BRIAN TRACY

Notes:

June

9

It takes strength to be gentle and kind.
STEVEN MORRISSEY

Notes:

June

10

Gratitude is the sweetest thing in a seeker's life – in all human life. If there is gratitude in your heart, then there will be tremendous sweetness in your eyes.

SRI CHINMOY

Notes:

June

11

The common denominator of success – the secret of success of every man who has ever been successful – lies in the fact that he formed the habit of doing things that failures don't like to do.

ALBERT GRAY

Notes:

June

12

Remember happiness doesn't depend upon who you are or what you have; it depends solely upon what you think.

DALE CARNEGIE

Notes:

June

13

The requisites of health are plain enough; regular habits, daily exercise, cleanliness, and moderation in all things – in eating as well as in drinking – would keep most people well.

JOHN LUBBOCK

Notes:

June

14

Home sweet home. This is the place to find happiness. If one doesn't find it here, one doesn't find it anywhere.

M. K. SONI

Notes:

June

15

Remember, as long as you live, that nothing but strict truth can carry you through the world, with either your conscience or your honor unwounded.
EARL OF CHESTERFIELD

Notes:

June

16

You can be deprived of your money, your job and your home by someone else, but remember that no one can ever take away your honor.

WILLIAM LYON PHELPS

Notes:

June

17

Hope is important because it can make the present moment less difficult to bear. If we believe that tomorrow will be better, we can bear a hardship today.

THICH NHAT HANH

Notes:

June

18

We come nearest to the great when we are great in humility.

RABINDRANATH TAGORE

Notes:

June

19

Among those whom I like or admire, I can find no common denominator, but among those whom I love, I can: all of them make me laugh.

W. H. AUDEN

Notes:

June

20

Nothing is more precious than independence and liberty.
HO CHI MINH

Notes:

June

21

Of all the things of a man's soul which he has within him, justice is the greatest good and injustice the greatest evil.
PLATO

Notes:

June 22

I expect to pass through life but once. If, therefore, there can be any kindness I can show, or any good thing I can do to any fellow human being, let me do it now.

WILLIAM PENN

Notes:

June

23

The more one knows, the less one knows.
LARRY JOHN PHILLIPS

Notes:

June

24

He has hard-working who has nothing to do.
PROVERB

Notes:

June

25

The journey, not the arrival, matters; the voyage, not the landing.

LOUIS THEROUX

Notes:

June

26

Tis better to have loved and lost, than never to have loved at all.
ALFRED TENNYSON

Notes:

June

27

There is one element that is worth its weight in gold and that is loyalty. It will cover a multitude of weaknesses.
PHILIP ARMOUR

Notes:

June

28

Maturity is when your world opens up and you realize that you are not the center of it.
M. J. CROAN

Notes:

June

29

I will not be a slave to myself, for it is a perpetual, a shameful, and the most heavy of all servitudes; and this end I may gain by moderate desires.
LUCIUS ANNAEUS SENECA

Notes:

June

30

Have a plan to earn money. Have a plan to carefully spend your money. Have a plan to save money. Have a plan to invest money.

ALFRED ARMAND MONTAPERT

Notes:

July

1

Circumstances may cause interruptions and delays, but never lose sight of your goal. Prepare yourself in every way you can by increasing your knowledge and adding to your experience, so that you can make the most of opportunity when it occurs.

MARIO ANDRETTI

Notes:

July

2

While we may not be able to control all that happens to us, we can control what happens inside us.
BENJAMIN FRANKLIN

Notes:

July

3

Nothing is particularly hard if you divide it into small jobs.
HENRY FORD

Notes:

July

4

To be able to look back upon one's past life with satisfaction is to live twice.
MARTIAL

Notes:

July

5

No great thing is created suddenly, more than a bunch of grapes or a fig. If you tell me that you desire a fig, I answer you that there must be time. Let it first blossom, then bear fruit, then ripen.
EPICTETUS

Notes:

July

6

Set peace of mind as your highest goal and organize your life around it.
ANONYMOUS

Notes:

July

7

A fool sees not the same tree that a wise man sees.
WILLIAM BLAKE

Notes:

July

8

With ordinary talent and extraordinary perseverance,
all things are attainable.
SIR THOMAS FOXWELL BUXTON

Notes:

July

9

Fall seven times, stand up eight.
JAPANESE PROVERB

Notes:

July

10

I know what pleasure is, for I have done good work.
ROBERT LOUIS STEVENSON

Notes:

July

11

Life itself is the most valuable thing any person possesses.

E. B. ZU TAVERN

Notes:

July

12

Without goals, and plans to reach them, you are like a ship that has set sail with no destination.
FITZHUGH DODSON

Notes:

July

13

Reputation is like fine china: Once broken it's very hard to repair.

ABRAHAM LINCOLN

Notes:

July

14

Respect yourself above all.
PYTHAGORAS

Notes:

July

15

The highest praise for a person is to give them responsibility.
SAYING

Notes:

July

16

Retirement is the last opportunity for individuals to reinvent themselves, let go of the past, and find peace and happiness within.

ERNIE J. ZELINSKI

Notes:

July 17

A man of knowledge uses words with restraint, and a man of understanding is even-tempered.
BIBLE

Notes:

July

18

Be the curator of your life. Slowly cut things out until you're left only with what you love, with what is necessary, with what makes you happy.

LEO BABAUTA

Notes:

July

19

Be sincere with your compliments. Most people can tell the difference between sugar and saccharine.

E. C. MCKENZIE

Notes:

July

20

Sit in solitude every day. Be quiet and be still. Calm your thoughts and get to know your inner voice.
JOHN SOFORIC

Notes:

July

21

Patience is a remedy for every sorrow.
PUBLIUS SYRUS

Notes:

July

22

From success you get a lot of things, but not that great inside thing that love brings you.
SAMUEL GOLDWYN

Notes:

July

23

Great souls suffer in silence.
FRIEDRICH SCHILLER

Notes:

July

24

Your talent is God's gift to you. What you do with it is your gift back to God.
LEO BUSCAGLIA

Notes:

July

25

All that we are is the result of what we have thought.
BUDDHA

Notes:

July

26

Every man's life lies within the present; for the past is spent and done with, and the future is uncertain.
MARCUS AURELIUS

Notes:

July

27

Tolerance is accepting differences in other people. It is thinking 'It is OK that you are different from me.

CYNTHIA AMOROSO

Notes:

July

28

Let your life reflect the faith you have in God. Fear nothing and pray about everything. Be strong, trust God's word, and trust the process.
GERMANY KENT

Notes:

July

29

The truth is always the strongest argument.
SOPHOCLES

Notes:

July

30

Wisdom comes alone through suffering.
AESCHYLUS

Notes:

July 31

Most people spend most of their days doing what they do not want to in order to earn the right, at times, to do what they may desire.
JOHN MASON BROWN

Notes:

August

1

Believe that pain is in the nature of life as is pleasure, and believe further that without struggle there can be no success either in achievement or character. Make trouble your friend. It will do something for your inner, emotional, psychic life that nothing else can possibly do.

JOHN MILLER

Notes:

August

2

Only years make men. Rarely do the great men of history distinguish themselves before they are fifty, and between fifty and eighty they do their best work – both as regards quality and quantity.

ADOLPH PHILIP GOUTHEY

Notes:

August

3

Keep away from those who try to belittle your ambitions. Small people always do that, but the really great make you believe that you, too, can become great.

MARK TWAIN

Notes:

August

4

When angry, count to four before you speak; if very angry, an hundred.
THOMAS JEFFERSON

Notes:

August

5

There is only one way to happiness and that is to cease worrying about things which are beyond the power of our will.
EPICTETUS

Notes:

August

6

Make it a habit to tell people thank you. To express your appreciation, sincerely and without the expectation of anything in return. Truly appreciate those around you, and you'll soon find many others around you. Truly appreciate life, and you'll find that you have more of it.

RALPH MARSTON

Notes:

August 7

Outer beauty turns the head, inner beauty turns the heart.

HELEN J. RUSSELL

Notes:

August

8

When I first open my eyes upon the morning meadows and look out upon the beautiful world, I thank God I am alive.
RALPH WALDO EMERSON

Notes:

August

9

You are the same today as you will be five years from now except for two things … the people you meet and the books you read.

CHARLES E. JONES

Notes:

August

10

Everyone wants to live on top of the mountain, but all the happiness and growth occurs while you're climbing it.

ANDY ROONEY

Notes:

August

11

The more tranquil a man becomes, the greater is his success, his influence, his power for good. Calmness of mind is one of the beautiful jewels of wisdom.
JAMES ALLEN

Notes:

August

12

Give us the fortitude to endure the things which cannot be changed, and the courage to change the things which should be changed, and the wisdom to know one from the other.
BISHOP OLIVER J. HART

Notes:

August

13

Man is buffeted by circumstances so long as he believes himself to be the creature of outside conditions, but when he realizes that he is a creative power, and that he may command the hidden soil and seeds of his being out of which circumstances grow, he then becomes the rightful master of himself.

JAMES ALLEN

Notes:

August

14

Conscience is the voice of the soul, the passions are the voice of the body.
JEAN-JACQUES ROUSSEAU

Notes:

August

15

Tis better to be lowly born, and range with humble livers in content, than to be perk'd up in a glistening grief, and wear a golden sorrow.
WILLIAM SHAKESPEARE

Notes:

August

16

A high heart ought to bear calamities and not flee them, since in bearing them appears the grandeur of the mind and in fleeing them the cowardice of the heart.

PIETRO ARETINO

Notes:

August 17

You can't live your life trying to please people. You be courteous, and you be respectful, but you've got to do things in the way that you want to do them.

KIP MOORE

Notes:

August

18

More decisions are dictated by human feelings than are made by logic and reason.
DR. PAUL PARKER

Notes:

August

19

Whatever you do, do it with determination. You have one life to live; do your work with passion and give your best. Whether you want to be a chef, doctor, actor, or a mother, be passionate to get the best result.

ALIA BHATT

Notes:

August 20

For whatever goal you want to achieve, there is discomfort along that path. Self-discipline drives you through this discomfort and allows you to achieve and attain. It's an essential component of mastery, and nothing great was ever accomplished without it.
PETER HOLLINS

Notes:

August 21

If a man empties his purse into his head, no man can take it away from him. An investment in knowledge always pays the best interest.
BENJAMIN FRANKLIN

Notes:

August

22

He who reigns himself and rules his passions, desires and fears is more than a king.
JOHN MILTON

Notes:

August 23

Every great and commanding movement in the annals of the world is the triumph of enthusiasm. Nothing great was ever achieved without it.

RALPH WALDO EMERSON

Notes:

August 24

They who say all men are equal speak an undoubted truth, if they mean all that have an equal right to liberty, to their property, and to their protection of the laws. But they are mistaken if they think men are equal in their station and employments, since they are not so by their talents.

VOLTAIRE

Notes:

August

25

Faith is staying focused on the positive and being grateful for what you have. Faith is trusting that the right answer to a problem will come to you – it's waiting patiently until things get resolved – knowing that prayer can be answered in many ways. All I have seen teaches me to trust the Creator for all I have not seen.

ANONYMOUS

Notes:

August

26

Forgiveness is not always easy. At times, it feels more painful than the wound we suffered, to forgive the one that inflicted it. And yet, there is no peace without forgiveness.

MARIANNE WILLIAMSON

Notes:

August

27

Liberty is one of the most valuable blessings that heaven has bestowed upon mankind.
MIGUEL DE CERVANTES

Notes:

August

28

It's no good trying to keep up friendships. It's painful for both sides. The fact is, one grows out of people, and the only thing is to face it.
WILLIAM SOMERSET MAUGHAM

Notes:

August

29

The way to wealth is as plain as the way to market. It depends on two words, industry and frugality: that is, waste neither time nor money, but make the best use of both. Without industry and frugality, nothing will do, and with them, everything.

BENJAMIN FRANKLIN

Notes:

August

30

Let him who would enjoy a good future waste none of the present.
ROGER BABSON

Notes:

August

31

He enjoys much who is thankful for little; a grateful mind is both a great and a happy mind.
THOMAS SECKER

Notes:

September 1

Successful people aren't born that way. They become successful by establishing the habits of doing things unsuccessful people don't like to do.
WILLIAM MAKEPEACE THACKERAY

Notes:

September

2

A happy life must be to a great extent a quiet life, for it is only in an atmosphere of quiet that true joy can live.

BERTRAND RUSSELL

Notes:

September

3

Health is a gift, but you have to work to keep it.
ELBERT HUBBARD

Notes:

September

4

There is nothing like staying at home for real comfort.
JANE AUSTEN

Notes:

September

5

If you tell the truth, you don't need a long memory.
JESSE VENTURA

Notes:

September

6

From our ancestors come our names, from our virtues our honors.
ANONYMOUS

Notes:

September

7

Hope is outreaching desire with expectancy of good.
It is characteristic of all living beings.
EDWARD S. AME

Notes:

September

8

An able yet humble man is a jewel worth a kingdom.
WILLIAM PENN

Notes:

September

9

One should take good care not to grow too wise for so great a pleasure of life as laughter.

JOSEPH ADDISON

Notes:

September 10

Independence is for the very few; it is a privilege of the strong.
FRIEDRICH NIETZSCHE

Notes:

September

11

It is not enough to have a good mind; the main thing is to use it well.
RENE DESCARTES

Notes:

September

12

The greatest thing a man can do for his heavenly Father is to be kind to some of his other children.
HENRY DRUMMOND

Notes:

September

13

It is not a question how much a man knows, but what use he can make of what he knows.

JOSIAH GILBERT HOLLAND

Notes:

September

14

What we do during our working hours determines what we have, what we do in our leisure hours determines what we are.

GEORGE EASTMAN

Notes:

September

15

A man can do nothing better than to eat and drink and find satisfaction in his work.
BIBLE

Notes:

September

16

Absence is to love what wind is to fire; it extinguishes the small, it enkindles the great.
COMTE DE BUSSY-RABUTIN

Notes:

September

17

Loyalty is one thing a leader cannot do without. It is as priceless as it is rare. It creates a quiet confidence in the heart of any leader and is the assurance of success in any enterprise.

ADOLPH PHILIP GOUTHEY

Notes:

September

18

Sometimes what we lack is the thrill of anticipation or the delay of gratification. We enjoy things far more when we've really desired them but had to wait for them. The real value is found in our self-control and patience, which allows to delay gratification and build anticipation. Letting desire build is an abstract way to achieve balance and moderation in your life…Moderation just may be the answer to boredom – go figure.

CRIS FRANK

Notes:

September

19

Regardless of one motives for amassing money, the results will not be what you hope for. Instead, the wise teachers of tradition tell us to go ahead and do the things we want and become good at them. In that lies our freedom.

MIKE PHILLIPS

Notes:

September

20

When opportunity presents itself, don't be afraid to go after it.

EDDIE KENNISON

Notes:

September

21

Optimism is the faith that leads to achievement.
Nothing can be done without hope and confidence.
HELEN KELLER

Notes:

September

22

For every minute spent in organizing, an hour is earned.
BENJAMIN FRANKLIN

Notes:

September

23

Trust God to weave your thread into the great web,
though the pattern shows it not yet.
GEORGE MACDONALD

Notes:

September

24

This is the gift that God reserves for his special proteges, talent and beauty he gives to many. Wealth is commonplace, fame not rare. But peace of mind – that is his final guerdon of approval, the fondest sign of his love. He bestows it. Most men are never blessed with it, others wait all their lives – yes, far into advanced age – for this gift to descend upon them.

JOSHUA LIEBMAN

Notes:

September

25

There is no failure except in no longer trying. There is no defeat except from within, no really insurmountable barrier save our own inherent weakness of purpose.
KIN HUBBARD

Notes:

September

26

If you don't know where you are going, how can you expect to get there?
BASIL S. WALSH

Notes:

September

27

A good name is seldom regained. When character is gone, all is gone, and one of the richest jewels of life is lost forever.

B. HEWES

Notes:

September

28

I see retirement as just another of these reinventions, another chance to do new things and be a new version of myself.
WALT MOSSBERG

Notes:

September

29

The great gift of conversation lies less in displaying it ourselves than in drawing it out of others. He who leaves your company pleased with himself and his own cleverness is perfectly well pleased with you.

JEAN DE LA BRUYERE

Notes:

September

30

Simplicity, simplicity, simplicity! I say, let your affairs be as two or three, and not a hundred or a thousand; instead of a million count half a dozen, and keep your accounts on your thumb-nail.

HENRY DAVID THOREAU

Notes:

October

1

Sincerity is the highest compliment you can pay.
RALPH WALDO EMERSON

Notes:

October

2

Heavy hearts, like heavy clouds in the sky, are best relieved by the letting of a little water.
CHRISTOPHER MORLEY

Notes:

October

3

There is only one success – to be able to spend your life in your own way.

CHRISTOPHER MORLEY

Notes:

October

4

You will never be any better or higher than your best thoughts.

ALFRED ARMAND MONTAPERT

Notes:

October

5

The value of time. What are friends, books or health, the interest of travel, or the delights of home, if we have not time for their employment.
JOHN LUBBOCK

Notes:

October

6

All I have seen teaches me to trust the creator for all I have not seen.

RALPH WALDO EMERSON

Notes:

October

7

Work expands so as to fill the time available for its completion.
C. NORTHCOTE PARKINSON

Notes:

October

8

The most disastrous times have produced the greatest minds. The purest metal comes of the most ardent furnace, the most brilliant lighting comes of the darkest clouds.

CHATEAUBRIAND

Notes:

October

9

If you do not have to worry about money matters, then old age may bring the joy of old books and old friends. If you love birds and animals, trees, grass, and blue skies – if you like good humor and beautiful pictures – then the hours may be brimful of golden happiness.

GRENVILLE KLEISER

Notes:

October

10

Consider what you have in the smallest chosen library. A company of the wisest and wittiest men that could be picked out of all civil countries, in a thousand years, have set in best order the results of their learning and wisdom. The men themselves were hid and inaccessible, solitary, impatient of interruption, fenced by etiquette; but the thought which they did not uncover to their bosom friend is here written out in transparent words to us, the strangers of another age.

RALPH WALDO EMERSON

Notes:

October

11

Learn to calm down the winds of your mind, and you will enjoy great inner peace.
REMEZ SASSON

Notes:

October

12

It is not the strongest of the species that survive, nor the most intelligent, but the one most responsive to change.

CHARLES DARWIN

Notes:

October

13

We can let circumstances rule us, or we can take charge and rule our lives from within.
EARL NIGHTINGALE

Notes:

October

14

Your success depends mainly upon what you think of yourself and whether you believe in yourself.
WILLIAM J. H. BOETCKER

Notes:

October 15

Content destroys all inordinate ambition; gives sweetness to the conversation, and serenity to all the thoughts; and if does not bring riches, it does the same thing by banishing the desire of them.
JAMES ADDISON

Notes:

October

16

I do not ask to walk smooth paths nor bear an easy load. I pray for strength and fortitude to climb the rock-strewn road. Give me such courage I can scale the hardest peaks alone, and transform every stumbling block into a steppingstone.

GAIL BROOK BURKET

Notes:

October

17

How sweet and gracious, even in common speech, is that fine sense which men call courtesy! Wholesome as air and genial as the light, welcome in every clime as breath of flowers, it transmutes aliens into trusting friends, and gives its owner a passport round the globe.
JAMES T. FIELDS

Notes:

October

18

The best we can do is size up the chances, calculate the risks involved, estimate our ability to deal with them, and then make our plans with confidence.

HENRY FORD

Notes:

October

19

Your ability to discipline yourself to set clear goals, and then to work toward them every day, will do more to guarantee your success than any other single factor.

BRIAN TRACY

Notes:

October

20

The greatest education to be had can be found in a library full of books. There, we can meet with those who are no longer alive, visit faraway places, relive history from a front row seat, listen to many of the greatest minds who have ever lived, take advice from the greatest of counselors, and learn from many of the world's greatest teachers; all in a lonely aisle flanked with some dusty old books.

J. S. FELTS

Notes:

October

21

The sign of an intelligent people is their ability to control their emotions by the application of reason.
MARYA MANNES

Notes:

October

22

Employ your time in improving yourself by other men's writings so that you shall come easily by what others have labored hard for.
SOCRATES

Notes:

October

23

Faith is no irresponsible shot in the dark. It is a responsible trust in God, who knows the desires of your hearts, the dreams you are given, and the goals you have set. He will guide your paths right.

ROBERT SCHULLER

Notes:

October 24

Friendship makes prosperity more brilliant, and lightens adversity by dividing and sharing it.
MARCUS TULLIUS CICERO

Notes:

October

25

If you do the very best you can, the future will take care of itself.
GEORGE MITCHELL

Notes:

October

26

It is always a good idea to be good and kind to yourself. Do whatever it takes to treat yourself with love and gentleness. You are a rare gem.

GIFT GUGU MONA

Notes:

October

27

That is not more pleasing exercise of the mind than gratitude.

JOSEPH ADDISON

Notes:

October

28

We become what we repeatedly do.
SEAN COVEY

Notes:

October

29

Happiness doesn't depend on any external
conditions, it is governed by our mental attitude.
DALE CARNEGIE

Notes:

October

30

Health squandered can never be compensated for by
the mere acquisition of money.
ORISON SWETT MARDEN

Notes:

October

31

No matter how big you are, when you go back home,
your family treats you like a normal person.
AJITH KUMAR

Notes:

November

1

This above all: to thine own self be true, and it must follow, as the night the day, thou canst not be false to any man.

WILLIAM SHAKESPEARE

Notes:

November

2

Without hope men are only half alive. With hope they dream and think and work.
CHARLES SAWYER

Notes:

November

3

The reward for humility and fear of the Lord is riches and honour and life.
BIBLE

Notes:

November

4

For health and the constant enjoyment of life, give me a keen and ever present sense of humor; it is the next best thing to an abiding faith in providence.
GEORGE B. CHEEVER

Notes:

November

5

It is better to have a fair intellect that is well-used
than a powerful one that is idle.
BRYANT H. MCGILL

Notes:

November

6

Kind words do not cost much. They never blister the tongue or lips. Mental trouble was never known to arise from such quarters. Though they do not cost much yet they accomplish much. They make other people good natured. They also produce their own image on men's souls, and a beautiful image it is.

BLAISE PASCAL

Notes:

November

7

The best day of your life is the one on which you decide your life is your own. No apologies or excuses. No one to lean on, rely on, or blame. The gift is yours – it is an amazing journey – and you alone are responsible for the quality of it. This is the day that your life rally begins.

BOB MOAWAB

Notes:

November

8

Women fall in love through their ears and men through their eyes.

WOODROW WYATT

Notes:

November

9

Too much work and too much energy kill a man just as effectively as too much-assorted vice or too much drink.

RUDYARD KIPLING

Notes:

November

10

Money is neither good or bad; it is the use of it which determines its value.
ALFRED ARMAND MONTAPERT

Notes:

November

11

Optimism inspires, energizes, and brings out our best. It points the mind toward possibilities and helps us think creatively past problems.
PRICE PRITCHETT

Notes:

November

12

I had no special sagacity, only the power of patient thought. I kept the subject constantly before me and waited until the first dawnings opened little by little into the full light.

ISAAC NEWTON

Notes:

November

13

There is no greater prize than a quiet, peaceful mind.
RASHEED OGUNLARU

Notes:

November

14

Most of the important things in the world have been accomplished by people who have kept on trying when there seemed to be no help at all.
ANDREW CARNEGIE

Notes:

November

15

If I take care of my character, my reputation will take care of me.
DWIGHT L. MOODY

Notes:

November

16

Retirement ... a time to experience a fulfilling life derived from many enjoyable and rewarding activities,
ERNIE J. ZELINSKI

Notes:

November

17

The good and the wise lead quiet lives.
EURIPIDES

Notes:

November

18

Ask how little, not how much, can I get along with. To say-is it necessary? – when I am tempted to add one more accumulation to my life, when I am pulled toward one more centrifugal activity.

ANNE MORROW LINDBERGH

Notes:

November

19

Without great solitude no serious work is possible.
PABLO PICASSO

Notes:

November 20

The great thing in this world is not so much where we stand as in what direction we are moving.
OLIVER WENDELL HOLMES

Notes:

November

21

To a great extent, suffering is a sort of need felt by the organism to make itself familiar with a new state, which makes it uneasy, to adapt its sensibility to that state.

MARCEL PROUST

Notes:

November

22

The pleasantest things in the world are pleasant thoughts; and the great art of life is to have as many of them as possible.
MICHEL DE MONTAIGNE

Notes:

November

23

The most important lesson that I learned is to trust God in every circumstance. Lots of times we go through difficult trials and following God's plan seems like it doesn't make any sense at all. God is always in control and he will never leave us.

ALLYSON FELIX

Notes:

November

24

I can't imagine anything more worthwhile than doing what I most love. And they pay me for it.
EDGAR WINTER

Notes:

November

25

Adversity does not break men; it makes them.
Opposition and failure bring out what is in man.
COUNCILLOR

Notes:

November

26

Each part of life has its own pleasures. Each has its own abundant harvest, to be garnered in season. We may grow old in body, but we need never grow old in mind and spirit. We must make a stand against old age. We must atone for its faults by activity. We must exercise the mind as we exercise the body, to keep it supple and buoyant. Life may be short, but it is long enough to live honorably and well. Old age is the consummation of life, rich in blessings.

MARCUS TULLIUS CICERO

Notes:

November

27

The beginning of anxiety is the end of faith, and the beginning of true faith is the end of anxiety.
GEORGE MULLER

Notes:

November

28

A positive attitude is definitely one of the keys to success. My definition of a positive attitude is a simple one: Looking for the good in all circumstances.

CATHERINE PULSIFER

Notes:

November

29

When you read the best books, you will have as the guests of your mind the best thoughts of the best men.

GRENVILLE KLEISER

Notes:

November

30

Calmness is a human superpower. The ability to not overreact or take things personally keeps your mind clear and heart at peace.

MARCANDANGEL

Notes:

December

1

Progress is impossible without change; and those who cannot change their minds cannot change anything.

GEORGE BERNARD SHAW

Notes:

December 2

The noblest contribution which any man can make for the benefit of posterity, is that of a good character. The richest bequest which any man can leave to the youth of his native land, is that of a shining, spotless example.

ROBERT C. WINTHROP

Notes:

December

3

Life is a matter of choices, and every choice you make makes you.
JOHN MAXWELL

Notes:

December 4

Good is the enemy of great. Greatness is not a function of circumstance. Greatness, it turns out, is largely a matter of conscious choice and discipline.

JAMES CHURTON COLLINS

Notes:

December

5

Conduct is the best proof of character.
ANONYMOUS

Notes:

December

6

We can accomplish almost anything within our ability if we but think that we can!
GEORGE MATTHEW ADAMS

Notes:

December

7

The rarity of happiness among those who achieved much is evidence that achievement is not in itself the assurance of a happy life. The great, like the humble, may have to find their satisfaction in the same plain things.

EDGAR ANDREW COLLARD

Notes:

December

8

You gain strength, courage, and confidence by every experience in which you really stop to look fear in the face. You must do the thing which you think you cannot do.

ELEANOR ROOSEVELT

Notes:

December

9

It is not death that a man should fear, but he should fear never beginning to live.
MARCUS AURELIUS

Notes:

December 10

Failure will never overtake me, if my determination to succeed is strong enough.
OG MANDINO

Notes:

December

11

Self-discipline is doing what needs to be done when it needs to be done when you don't feel like doing it.
ANONYMOUS

Notes:

December

12

Until you learn to control your emotions, you will never control your life.

J. S. FELTS

Notes:

December

13

When you have faith in God, you don't have to worry about the future. You just know it's all in his hands. You just go and do your best.
ELDER BYRAN MATHISON

Notes:

December

14

I keep my friends as misers do their treasures,
because, of all the things granted us by wisdom,
none is greater or better than friendship.
PIETRO ARETINO

Notes:

December

15

The root of joy is gratefulness.
DAVID STEINDL-RAST

Notes:

December

16

You'll never change your life until you change something you do daily. The secret of your success is found in your daily routine.
JOHN MAXWELL

Notes:

December

17

Our greatest happiness does not depend on the condition of life in which chance has placed us, but is always the result of a good conscience, good health, occupation and freedom in all just pursuits.
THOMAS JEFFERSON

Notes:

December

18

It is certain that tis easier to preserve Health than to recover it, and to prevent Diseases than to cure them.

DR. GEORGE CHEYNE

Notes:

December

19

Life imposes things on you that you can't control, but you still have the choice of how you are going to live through this.

CELINE DION

Notes:

December

20

The use of money is all the advantage there is in having money.

BENJAMIN FRANKLIN

Notes:

December

21

Rush is the enemy of growth. Leaf by leaf, the great oak grows into a sturdy tree. Forty years alone in the desert produced a Moses. Three years alone in the Arabian desert perfected Paul's vision and thought, made him a world citizen.

ADOLPH PHILIP GOUTHEY

Notes:

December

22

You will find peace not by trying to escape problems, but by confronting them courageously. You will find peace not in denial, but in victory.

B. DONALD WALTERS

Notes:

December

23

I have learned that success is to be measured not by the position that one has reached in life as by the obstacles which he has overcome while trying to succeed.

BOOKER T. WASHINGTON

Notes:

December

24

You can do what you want to do, accomplish what you want to accomplish, attain any reasonable objective you may have in mind…Not all of a sudden, perhaps, not in on one swift and sweeping act of achievement… But you can do it gradually – day by day and play by play – if you want to do it, if you will to do it, if you work to do it, over a sufficiently long period of time.

WILLIAM E. HOLLER

Notes:

December

25

With the new day comes new strength and new thoughts.

ELEANOR ROOSEVELT

Notes:

December

26

Finally, brothers, whatever is true, whatever is noble, whatever is right, whatever is pure, whatever is lovely, whatever is admirable if anything is excellent or praiseworthy think about such things.

BIBLE

Notes:

December

27

You can only become truly accomplished at something you love. Don't make money your goal. Instead, pursue the things you love doing, and then do them so well that people can't take their eyes off you.

MAYA ANGELOU

Notes:

December

28

All things that we see standing accomplished in the world are properly the outer material result, the practical realization and embodiment of thoughts that dwell in the great men sent into the world.

THOMAS CARLYLE

Notes:

December

29

Every man must go through the fire. This means that during your lifetime you will experience great suffering or great sorrow, and you will need the help of God to win over your problems.

ALFRED ARMAND MONTAPERT

Notes:

December

30

Whatever the mind of man can conceive and believe,
it can achieve.
NAPOLEON HILL

Notes:

December

31

A strong will, a settled purpose, an invincible determination, can accomplish almost anything; and in this lies the distinction between great men and little men.

THOMAS FULLER

Notes:

About the Author

Born and raised in northeastern Indiana, Larry John Phillips is married with 2 children and 5 grandchildren. He is a semi-retired business owner with a B.S. degree from Purdue University. During his free time, in addition to collecting quotations, Larry enjoys playing golf, gardening and spending time at their lake cottage with family.

During the last 40 years, Larry collected quotations on different topics and formed a habit of reflecting on them as part of his morning routine. Over the years he continued to expand the collection of his favorite quotations and today it consists of over 100 topics and 2,500 quotations. The journey with quotations has had a profound, uplifting, and thought-provoking impact on his life.

www.ingramcontent.com/pod-product-compliance
Lightning Source LLC
LaVergne TN
LVHW081314110826
845149LV00006B/1502

* 9 7 8 1 9 5 8 6 4 0 8 7 6 *